Bilbao

Editorial Everest would like to thank you for purchasing this book. It has been created by an extensive and complete publishing team made up of photographers, illustrators and authors specialised in the field of tourism, together with our modern cartography department. Everest guarantees that the contents of this work were completely up to date at the time of going to press, and we would like to invite you to send us any information that helps us to improve our publications, so that we may always offer QUALITY TOURISM.

Please send your comments to:
Editorial Everest. Dpto. de Turismo
Apartado 339 – 24080 León (Spain)
Or e-mail them to us at turismo@everest.es

The whole world is a bigger Bilbao.

(Miguel de Unamuno)

Editorial Management: Raquel López Varela

Editorial coordination: Aizkorri argitaletxea

Text: Xabi Larrañaga Muñoz

Diagrams: José Manuel Núñez

Photographs: Mikel Alonso, Gonzalo M. Azumendi, Santiago Yaniz Aramendia,
Iñaki Aguirre and Archivo Everest

Photographs of the Guggenheim Museum: Mikel Alonso and Santiago Yaniz
© FMGB Guggenheim Bilbao Museoa.

Cover design: Francisco A. Morais

Digital image processing: David Aller

Cartography: © EVEREST

Translated by: EURO:TEXT

SECOND EDITION
© EDITORIAL EVEREST, S. A.
Carretera León-La Coruña, km 5 – LEÓN
ISBN: 978-84-241-0137-4
Legal deposit: LE. 812-2007
Printed in Spain

EDITORIAL EVERGRÁFICAS, S. L.
Carretera León-La Coruña, km 5
LEÓN (Spain)

Classic view of Bilbao during the 18th century as depicted in a drawing by Thomas Moroney 1784.

THE OLD BILBAO - EL VIEJO BILBAO

The official history of Bilbao started more than seven centuries ago, on 15th June, 1300. Diego López de Haro, Lord of Vizcaya, signed Bilbao's Town Charter in Valladolid. The very small population was, at that time, distributed along both banks of the Estuary. The left bank, known today as *Bilbao La Vieja* (Old Bilbao), was where miners and their families lived. Diego López de Haro chose the right bank, inhabited by a few fishermen, to establish the new town.

Three streets, Somera, Artecall and Tendería, formed the first urban nucleus which could be accessed through two gates: Atxuri, which faced Durango and Balmaseda and Zamudio, which faced the Asua Valley. One century later, the people of Bilbao (Bilbainos), of whom there were fewer than two thousand, took charge of the building project for the Church of Santiago, which is now a cathedral.

By that time, rapid economic and demographic growth of the area was the reason for further expansion to include four new streets: Belosticalle, Carnicería Vieja, Barrencalle and Barrencalle Barrena. This was how the so-called *Siete Calles* (Seven Streets) came into being, the core of what is now called the **Casco Viejo** (Old Quarter).

El Arenal Bridge in 1878. Postcard from that period.

Church of Saint Antón and its bridge in the 19th century. Engraving by J. E. Delmas.

The Old Quarter is the sum of these Seven Streets and those which followed in the direction of **El Arenal.** The catastrophic floods of 1983, when the water level rose various metres, meant that it had to be renovated. It boasts more than 800 shops and 200 bars and restaurants. The best way to see it is starting from the **Puente de San Antón** which joins both banks of the Estuary. This bridge used to be the entrance point for Castilian wool and the exit point for manufactured products originating from Europe. It had three eyes and has been reconstructed several times in the intervening centuries. Next to the bridge stands the **Church of San Antón,** built in the 15th century on a fortress which, along with the bridge, is included on the town's coat of arms. It is a gothic temple, with an almost square floor plan, with three naves divided into four sections. Its main doorway, from the renaissance, and its tower in a Churrigueresque style, capped by a weather vane are worthy of note. The upper level of the portico was used by the authorities for presiding over public events which were held in the **Plaza Vieja,** located in the area which today accommodates the **Mercado de la Ribera.**

View of Bilbao's Old Quarter.

Ribera Bridge.

◀ *Church of Saint Antón.*

*Market stained glass window
with the town coat of arms.*

This market hall was built at the beginning of the 20th century and in 1990 was acknowledged by Guinness World Records as the most complete local market. It is also the largest covered market in Europe. A browse round its vegetable and fish stalls enlightens the visitor as to the extraordinary quality of Basque cuisine. Moreover, it is occasionally used for various cultural events such as fashion and theatre shows. The Old Quarter can be accessed via Calle Ronda. No. 16 of this street was the birthplace of Miguel de Unamuno. Ronda was originally outside the urban heart. It was from here that the entrance to the town was guarded and remains of the wall can still be seen today in the alley Cantón de Camarón. Calle Somera, characterised by high buildings due to the scarcity of land for building, can

Ribera Market, built in approximately 1920 on the original port quays.

Paintings on the ceiling of the Ribera Arches.

Naja Quays opposite the Old Quarter.

be reached via this alley. The passage of history and, in particular, the bombardments during the second Carlista War, have erased almost all medieval remnants. This is a typical area for having tapas and drinks in various bars which is referred to as *tapeo* and *chiquiteo* respectively, a very popular custom amongst the Bilbainos. Alongside door number 12 is a plaque indicating this as the birthplace of the musician Juan Crisóstomo de Arriaga.

Tendería is reached by crossing Artecalle via Cantón Alejandro de la Sota. This is where the **Church of Santiago** is located. It was awarded the status of **cathedral** in 1950 and represents the most important religious building in Bilbao. From the start of its construction in 1379 it has been a key stop along The Coastal Section of the Pilgrim's Route to Santiago. Its tremendous portico was started in 1571 and was, at the same time, used as a buttress, cemetery and covered market.

The Angel's Door, in the cathedral, used by pilgrims of The Coastal Way of St. James.

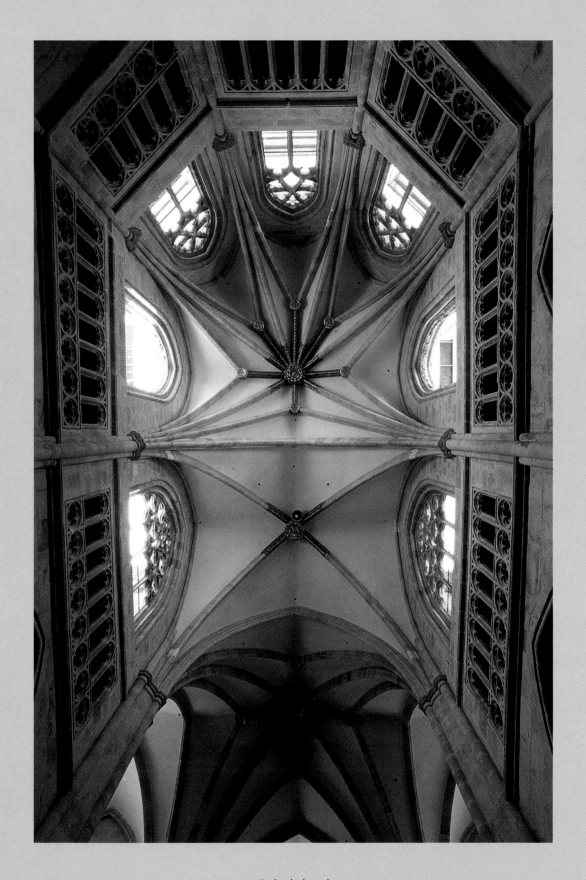

Cathedral vault.

Cathedral gothic cloister.

Solemn mass concelebrated in the Cathedral during the reopening of the temple to worship following its full restoration in 2000.

◀ *Neogothic tower and façade of the Cathedral.*

► *Archaeological, Ethnographical and Basque Historical Museum. Cloister and "Mikeldi", the enigmatic prehistoric idol.*

Church of Saints Juanes.

The interior with its three naves is worth a visit, the ambulatory and the triforium are outstanding. The main doorway is the work of Severino de Achúcarro, neogothic in style, and looks onto a small square dominated by the baroque **Fountain of Santiago,** designed in 1785 by the artist Luis Paret. At one side of the cathedral, on the **Puerta del Ángel** (The Angel's Door) from 1515, a pilgrim's shell can be observed, emphasising how significant Bilbao has been for The Way of St. James. It is not in vain that the Apostle St. James the Elder has been Patron Saint of the town since 1643.

The **Portal de Zamudio** (Gate of Zamudio) is a few steps away and was the entrance for rural products to the town. In days gone by, this entrance was defended by a tower which was later converted into a prison. The nearby **Santos Juanes Church** possesses remarkable baroque altarpieces. The Jesuits had rooms at the rear which stood round a cloister with three floors. This is currently home to the **Basque Museum,** where historical, ethnographical and anthropological exhibitions are organised.

*Mausoleum of the powerful Bilbao family,
the Arana-Varonas in the Cathedral.*

Ascent to Begoña using the Mallona Steps.

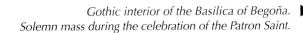
It is constantly undergoing a process of renovation, however one of the objects always worth visiting is the *Mikeldi,* the stone block in the shape of a pig or wild boar, elaborated during the Iron Age. It has a large disc under its stomach and has to be considered as a distant relation of the Bull of Guisando. The museum also has various objects from the everyday history of the Basques.

The **Plaza de Unamuno** has a bust of the writer, the entrance to the Metro and the start of the **Calzadas de Mallona** (Mallona Steps) which linked the town with the Anteiglesia de Begoña (Parish of Begoña). The stairs lead to the **Basilica,** gothic in style and built in 1519. It is also possible, and more comfortable, to go up to Begoña using the lift located in Calle Esperanza behind the **Church of San Nicolás.** The Basilica's main doorway is plateresque and both the Basilica and the Virgin to which it is dedicated are much

Basilica of Begoña, home to the patron saint of Vizcaya, the Virgin of Begoña.

loved and revered by the people of Vizcaya. At number 7 Calle de la Cruz, next to Plaza de Unamuno is where the writer lived as a child and in the house opposite, number 6, is where José Antonio de Aguirre y Lekube, the first Lehendakari (Basque President) of the Basque Government, was born.

Plaza Nueva is a few metres away, similar to other arcades such as the Plaza Mayor in Madrid or Salamanca. Designed in the 18th century and completed a century later, it soon became the recreational centre of the town. One of its buildings acts as the headquarters of **Euskaltzaindia,** the Academy of the Basque Language and its porticos are used to hold the Sunday market of books, stamps, birds, etc. and an array of activities during the August fiestas known as *Aste Nagusia*. It is a stopping place for those who wish to sample the typical *pintxos* (elaborate tapas) or relax on a terrace.

One of the entrances leads to the **Church of Saint Nicolás** which was a fishermen's chapel in the middle ages. In 1754, Ignacio Ibero took charge of the construction of a house of God, the original floor plan of which was octagonal. Inside there are five magnificent altarpieces by the sculptor Juan de Mena. The façade, next to the entrance, bears a commemorative plaque indicating the level reached by the floods of 1983. Next to the church is the **Palacio Gómez de la Torre,** a neoclassic palace dating back to the end of the 18th century, and at the rear in Calle Esperanza, is the aforementioned lift which goes as far as Begoña.

Main doorway of Saint Nicolás, baroque temple with an octagonal floor plan (18th century).

Saint Nicolás Square.

Flower market in El Arenal.

Tranquillity in the El Arenal gardens.

In front of the Church of Saint Nicolás are gardens called **El Arenal,** which stretch from the **Teatro Arriaga** (Arriaga Theatre) to the **Town Hall of Bilbao.** These gardens used to be a beach, hence their name *(El Arenal,* The Sandy Area), then quay and from the 18th century a place for recreation, shaded with acacias and lime trees. On Sundays a flower market is held in **El Arenal** and a modernist concert is given by the Municipal Band on the *kiosko* (bandstand). On one Saturday of each month, it is also customary to have a display of traditional Basque dances in which anyone who wishes can participate. During the summer fiestas, El Arenal is full of *txosnas,* the popular marquees with music.

Dome of the La Unión y Fénix building beside El Arenal.

El Arenal promenade.

The **Arriaga Theatre** was built in 1890 and is named after the local composer Juan Crisóstomo de Arriaga, who died aged 19 and who was, nevertheless, considered "the Spanish Mozart" at the beginning of the 19th century. The building is the work of Joaquín Rucoba, who also built the **Casa Consistorial** (Town Hall) and reminiscent of the Paris Opera House. It is spectacular inside. Like almost all of the Old Quarter, it was renovated after the last floods and since then has invited the best companies on the theatre circuit. In front of the theatre is a typical Bilbao café, **Café Boulevard.**

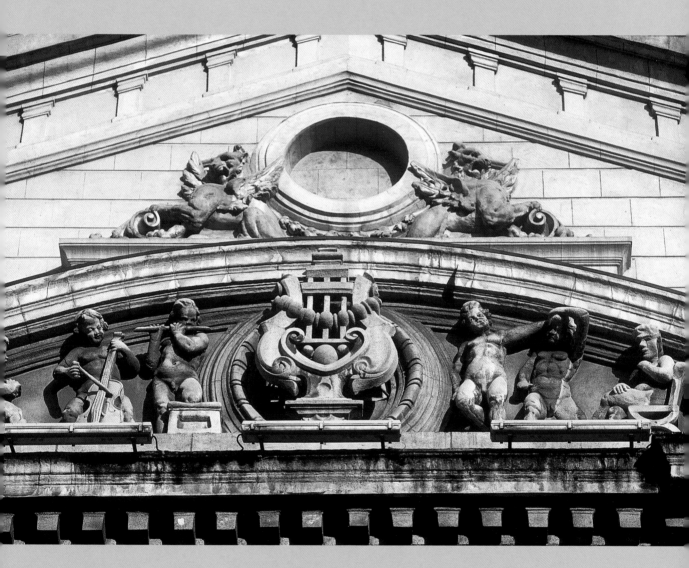

Arriaga Theatre. Top, views of the rear façade;
left, telamones on the side façade.

Double page overleaf: Arriaga Theatre at night.

Bourgeois architecture along the Calle del Correo.

One of Bilbao's Seven Streets or Old Quarter.

Two roads which are vital for local business end at **El Arenal:** the streets known as Bidebarrieta and Correo. These form part of the old zone which grew outside the town walls and in the former there are impressive palaces worth mentioning such as the **Mazarredo Palace,** which is adorned with a huge coat of arms. This is the street where the **Municipal Library** can be found, designed by the architect Severino de Achúcarro. It was built at the end of the 19th century to accommodate the headquarters of the society **El Sitio** which commemorates the blockade suffered by the town during the last Carlista War. It is one of Bilbao's most important cultural centres. The Calle Correo links **El Arenal** and the **Cathedral of Santiago.** Other sights worthy of mention on the same street are the neoclassic **Gortazar Palace** and the baroque **Allendesalazar Palace.**

*Municipal library:
auditorium and stained
glass window.*

The well-liked Dog Fountain in the old Bilbao.

Very close, stands the **Palacio de los Vargas,** (Palace of the Vargas Family) which dates back to the 17th century. It is located in the Calle de la Torre and now houses **the Stock Exchange.** Opposite the entrance, a mark on the ground indicates the exact place from where the **Begoña Basilica** can be seen in the distance. It is also worth stopping at the **Fuente del Perro** from 1800, in the neighbouring Calle del Perro. This fountain is neoclassic in style and its name, which was eventually given to the entire street, is the source of legendary confusion: the heads over which the water flows are not dogs but lions.

Partial view of Bilbao with the Arriaga Theatre in the foreground.

Façade of the Allendesalazar Palace.

THE NEW BILBAO - EL ENSANCHE

The population of Bilbao grew constantly from its founding up
to the end of the 19th century, point in time when an extremely
sharp increase began. In 1880 it had 11,000 inhabitants and
only two decades later this figure had multiplied by seven.
Workers from all over Spain immigrated, drawn by the
economic development of Bilbao and its surroundings, and in
a very short space of time there was a dramatic change in the
social and urban physiognomy. It was an era characterised by
momentous historical events such as the *Zamacolada*, the
occupation of the town by Napoleonic troops and, above all,
the Carlista Wars. Bilbao suffered various blockades and since
then is renowned for being a liberal town.

The Estuary adapted itself to circumstances: the company
Ferrocarril Bilbao-Tudela (Bilbao-Tudela Railway) was
founded in 1857. The **Banco de Bilbao** (Bank of Bilbao)
was created in the same year, in 1882 the steel foundry
Altos Hornos and in 1891 the commodities exchange was
put into operation. One year later the **Town Hall** was
inaugurated and in 1897 the **Escuela de Ingenieros** (College
of Engineers) opened.

Façade of the Stock Exchange.

El Arenal Bridge links Old Bilbao to the new town, El Ensanche.

All of the above made the enlargement of the town towards the other side of the river Nervión essential. The Seven Streets and the surroundings were not sufficient to respond to new demands. In 1876, the El Ensanche project was approved in which the following architects participated: Severino de Achúcarro, Ernesto Hoffmeyer and Pablo de Alzola. At the beginning of the 20th century, Bilbao ceased to be a dark labyrinth of intertwining narrow streets and spread out towards the areas of Abando, Begoña, Deusto and even Erandio.

From the Seven Streets the other side of the Estuary is reached by crossing the **Puente del Arenal.** After the floods, referred to as the *aguaduchus,* the Carlista Wars and the Civil War, little was left of the first bridge, christened with the name of Isabel II in 1845. It had a bascule section that could be raised and lowered to allow ships to pass. Immediately after crossing the bridge on the left is the **Railway Station,** the popular **Tren de la Robla** (Robla Train), which was of paramount importance for the economic and demographic growth of the town.

A little further ahead are the headquarters of the **Sociedad Bilbaína,** a bourgeois club copied from the English clubs. Its members usually met in Plaza Nueva, however in 1913 they decided to move to the other side of the Estuary. The building was designed by the architect Emiliano Amann and is Viennese in style. Its interior is outstanding for its magnificence. It boasts a splendid library and a wonderful collection of Basque paintings.

The **Official Commodities Exchange** stands right next to the **Sociedad Bilbaína.** There used to be stockbrokers in the Boulevard, the Arriaga, Plaza Nueva and in the Banco de Bilbao de San Nicolás, however with the new century they also turned their attention to the other side of the Nervión. In 1905 they inaugurated their own headquarters behind the **Estación del Norte** (North Station), also referred to as the **Estación de Abando.** This was where the first fixed Bilbao bullring was, apart from the one which used to be erected in days gone by next to Saint Antón. The current bullring, Plaza de Vista Alegre, was inaugurated in 1882 and, after suffering a severe fire, rebuilt in 1962.

Continuing upwards takes the visitor to the **Plaza Circular,** the starting point for the main avenues of El Ensanche. On one side is **Abando Station,** a vital communications link and the future location of the **Estación Intermodal** (Intermodal Station). This is where local and national trains arrive as well as the metro which links the centre with the neighbourhoods and with the municipalities of the **Greater Bilbao.**

This artistic glazing, which dominates the platforms of Abando Station or North Station, summarises the town's history.

Main hall of Abando Station or North Station.

Monument to Diego López de Haro, founder of the town.

Façades of the Circular Square.

Alameda de Mazarredo. French style bourgeois homes.

Albia Gardens.

There is also a tram stop very nearby. The station is overlooked by one of the highest and emblematic buildings, the BBV (Banco Bilbao Vizcaya). On the other side of the square is the **Café La Granja,** the place for gatherings, rendezvous and business meetings.

Plaza Circular is overlooked from his pedestal by Diego López de Haro, the founder of the town who is seen holding the Town Charter in his right hand. This is the starting point of Bilbao's main avenue, the **Gran Vía,** in the heart of the new town. To the left and right are outstanding buildings which are proof of Bilbao's economic strength. It is worth strolling from the **Plaza Circular** to the **Plaza del Sagrado Corazón,** at the other end of Gran Vía, to enjoy the elegant palaces, the majority of which are in the hands of public institutions.

The first urbanised square of El Ensanche was **Los Jardines de Albia,** a few metres away from the Gran Vía. Today these gardens represent a small, tree-lined oasis in the middle of buzzing business. They have the statues of Antonio de Trueba, *Antón el de los Cantares,* and Sabino Arana. The first was a costumbrismo writer during the 19th century and the second founder of the PNV, the Basque Nationalist Party. The house of his birth was nearby, however was demolished and the same ground was used to build *Sabin Etxea,* the PNV's headquarters. This is also the location of the **Palacio de Justicia** (Lawcourts) and **San Vicente Mártir,** the old parish of the Anteiglesia de Abando. It was founded in 1190, rebuilt during the 16th century and reformed during the 19th century. Its side doorway is gothic from the 14th century. It has three naves, and Antonio Trueba is buried here in a tomb in the wall.

Façade of the building Casa Montero.

View of the Gran Vía.

Next to San Vicente is one of the town's most representative entertainment venues, the **Kafe Antzokia.** Inaugurated in 1995 with the intention of promoting Basque culture, it organises hundreds of concerts of all types. It is also one of the most visited venues during festivals or at night by Bilbainos. On the other side of the Albia Gardens is the **Iruña,** a traditional café and restaurant "since time immemorial". Going back to the **Gran Vía,** the visitor crosses Calle Ledesma, another typical venue for *chiquiteo.*

Walking to **Plaza del Sagrado Corazón,** there is an abundance of splendid buildings such as the old **Banco de Bilbao,** the **Palacio de la Diputación Foral** (Regional Council Offices) and in the **Plaza Elíptica,** or Plaza Moyúa, stands the **Palacio de Chávarri** (Chávarri Palace), the headquarters of the Civil Government. The **Carlton Hotel** is also in this square which, during the 1936 War, gave shelter to the Basque Government presided over by the Lehendakari Aguirre.

Two views of the Banco Bilbao façade. ▶

Beautiful façade in Bilbao's Gran Vía.

Main hall of the Carlton Hotel (1927).

Standing in the centre of the square and looking into the distance, in any direction, it is obvious why Bilbao is referred to as *El Botxo* (the hole): it is an urban conglomeration surrounded by hills, almost squeezed in between them. Seven hills surround and protect it. The most popular of these is Artxanda. The easiest and most attractive way of getting to the top of Artxanda is using the funicular railway which gradually reveals the town during its ascent. Once at the top, you can delight in a panoramic view of Bilbao and its surroundings. Many Bilbainos visit it at the weekends to stroll, eat or enjoy the views.

Top, Artxanda funicular railway with ▶
the Ciudad Jardín in the background.

Bottom, Federico Moyua Square
or Elliptic Square.

◀ *Two views of the Bilbao Park or Doña Casilda Park.*

Section of the Zuloaga monument.

A few metres from Moyúa Square is the **Parque de Doña Casilda.** For a long time it was the main, and almost only, green oasis in the town until other huge parks were created such as **Parque de Europa** in Txurdinaga, **Parque de la Peña** or **Parque de Etxebarria** located between the Seven Streets and Begoña. This clear commitment to improving the quality of life of its inhabitants is one of the most marked changes to affect the new Bilbao. In 2002 a private study qualified its "green urban area" as the best equipped in Spain with regard to cleaning services, accesses, bicycle lanes, sport areas, swings etc. In this regard, the **Parque de Doña Casilda,** which today is still known as *El Parque* without having to use it full name, was very much on its own in the past. It is a place for recreation and relaxation with ponds, sculptures, secluded corners, silent strolls and a play area for children. *La Pérgola* in the park is used as a venue for various concerts during the August festivities. It is also home to the recently reformed **Museo de Bellas Artes** (Museum of Fine Arts), which has experienced an exceptional growth in interest with the creation of the **Guggenheim Museum.**

Autumn in Bilbao Park.

Section of the monument to Doña Casilda de Iturrizar, after which the park is named. ▶

Museum of Fine Arts from the outside.

Bilbao's Museum of Fine Arts has been the town's hidden jewel for many decades and owes its foundation in 1914 to the initiative of the Diputación de Vizcaya (Government of Vizcaya), the Ayuntamiento de Bilbao (Bilbao Council) and various other local collectors. It was created during a period of social and cultural modernisation with the intention of giving the artistic community exemplary models for their training. It was supervised by the painter Manuel Losada and, initially, was set up in the Escuela de Artes y Oficios in **Atxuri** near the Seven Streets.

He soon began to receive generous donations and bequests from institutions and private individuals and, a decade later, his success encouraged the creation of a second museum dedicated to contemporary art. This **Museo de Arte Moderno,** located in offices belonging to the Council, was supervised by the painter Aurelio Arteta.

Once the Civil War had come to an end it was decided to design a new area to unite the collections of both museums in the new part of the town.

Neoclassic in style, according to the project of the architects Fernando Urrutia and Gonzalo Cárdenas, the building was inaugurated in 1945 and declared a Monument of Historical-Artistic Importance in 1962. After various remodelling measures and enlargements, in 1991 the Basque Government entered to form part of the Museum and, under the management of Miguel Zugaza, a magnificent transformation took place which led to it being reinaugurated in 2001. It is home to one of the best art galleries in Spain and is a must for anyone wishing to delight in Basque painting.

Its permanent collection includes works by Diego de la Cruz, El Greco, Anton Van Dyck, Martin de Vos, Bartolomé Esteban Murillo, Francisco de Zurbarán, Francisco de Goya, Paul Gauguin, Paul Cézanne, Darío de Regoyos, Ignacio Zuloaga, Joaquín Sorolla, José Gutiérrez Solana, Aurelio Arteta, Jorge Oteiza, Eduardo Chillida, Antoni Tàpies, etc. Its temporary exhibitions are also superb.

A room with classic Spanish paintings.

Bottom, main entrance of the Museum of Fine Arts.

BILBAO IN THE 21ST CENTURY

In 1988 the town chronicler Luis del Olmo entitled one of his books as: *Bilbao, cómo has cambiao (Bilbao, how you've changed).* Nobody could have imagined what was to come, the magnificent transformation which is the pride of its inhabitants and astonishing to visitors. In honour of a known saying, Bilbao was strong in the face of adversity and took advantage of two disasters which occurred during the last quarter of the 20th century to bring out its best: on the one hand, the terrible floods gave impetus to the renovation of the most damaged part of the town, the Seven Streets and the surrounding area. On the other hand, the industrial restructuring made the town reinvent itself both on an urban and social level.

Many Bilbaínos initially viewed the institutional challenge with mistrust and incredulity. Projects such as the **Metro** and the **Guggenheim Museum** sparked great controversy and only their indisputable success has put an end to the majority of the criticisms. Bilbao immediately began to fill with tourists and prominent visitors who were accompanied by many international hotel chains, luxury restaurants, upmarket clothes and accessories shops, etc. Thus the change in the town's appearance also led to a change of mentality in its inhabitants. Initial discouragement and indifference has given way to a healthy and stimulating pride. Although there is still a quite melancholic feeling with regard to that grey Bilbao of bygone years, almost no one feels a real desire to go back to these times anymore.

Detail of the façade of the Hespería Hotel Bilbao.

Double page overleaf, an entrance to Bilbao's metro, designed by Norman Foster.

Gran Hotel Domine Bilbao Silken.

University of Deusto.

Out of necessity the port area, **Abandoibarra,** was restructured and turned into an area for recreation, leisure and services. In the space of a few years, various hotels, shopping centres, play areas for children and three bridges: **Euskalduna, Pasarela del Padre Arrupe** and **Zubi-Zuri** by Santiago Calatrava have been built along the Estuary as well as a magnificent promenade along the Nervión. This area, from Olabeaga to El Arenal, can be seen by foot or from the tram, the latter being another of the recent developments incorporated into Bilbao's landscape. The future of **Abandoibarra's** central esplanade is undoubtedly promising: it is planned to form a stunning cultural triangle composed of the **Guggenheim Museum,** the new library of the **University of Deusto,** designed by Rafael Moneo and the **Auditorium of the University of the Basque Country,** by the architect Alvaro Siza.

Euskalduna Bridge links the Deusto riverbank with Doña Casilda Park.

Two important buildings, flanking each side of the **Museum of Fine Arts,** represent the pinnacle of this revolutionary change: the **Palacio Euskalduna** and the **Guggenheim Museum.**
The **Palacio Euskalduna de Congresos y de la Música,** a congress centre and auditorium, is located at the west end of the Parque de Doña Casilda. It symbolises the last ship built in the shipyard and was designed by the architects Federico Soriano and Dolores Palacios. It was inaugurated in 1999, has various areas and hosts a multitude of activities. Its artistic programme includes dance, theatre, opera and modern music events. In 2003 it was given an award for the best Congress Centre in the world.

Two views of Euskalduna Palace.

Another view of the Euskalduna Palace and the Euskotran.

The **Guggenheim Museum** is the flagship of Bilbao's transformation. The process for its construction started in 1991. Two years later the foundation stone was laid and in 1997 the impressive building designed by Frank O.Gehry was inaugurated. *Puppy,* an enormous floral dog by Jeff Koons, welcomes visitors to the museum. According to a local joke, which is telling with regard to the character of the Bilbainos, the museum is merely the kennel for this appealing pooch. Behind the museum, along the promenade, pedestrians can walk under the legs of the bronze *Mamá,* from the *Araña* (Spider) series by Louise Bourgeois. It is also considerable in size.

The building is made of a series of interconnected volumes, clad in limestone with titanium sheathing. Added to this is glass, curvilinear and twisted shapes, and the overall effect is breathtaking. Depending on the time of day, light is reflected differently on its structures and the museum itself, gigantic, is fully reflected on the water of the Nervión. If possible, it is also worth seeing it at night, from the **Deusto Bridge.**

Its spectacular interior consists of 19 galleries. One of these is 130 metres long and 30 metres wide, without columns, the ideal exhibition room for works of art which would otherwise be difficult to fit into the usual rooms. Its collection and exhibitions attract thousands of visitors and the museum adds lustre to the daily life of Bilbainos since it is used for presentations and various social events.

Two photographs of the Guggenheim reflected in the Estuary.

Outside and inside
the Guggenheim
Museum in Bilbao.

Abandoibarra and
Guggenheim
Museum riverside
walk.

Surroundings of the Guggenheim (previous page) and
part of the outside of the building.

Two views of Bilbao's Maritime Museum.

By walking from the **Guggenheim Museum** towards the coast, the visitor quickly comes across *Bilbao's Maritime Museum* **(Museo Marítimo Ría de Bilbao),** another of the town's innovations. It was inaugurated at the end of 2003 and is built upon an immense area which accommodated the docks for the Euskalduna shipyards prior to the restructuring. The **Carola Crane,** commemorates and symbolises an era of a not so distant past and its interior is divided into three large thematic blocks: The Nervión and its banks as a maritime port, as a market and factory and as a naval shipyard. It provides information regarding both the physical changes in the area as well as the social and cultural changes driven by the economic activity in the Estuary.

Ametzola, a new area of Bilbao built on the land of the old freight station.

Nevertheless, the new part of Bilbao comprises much more than the rehabilitated area of Abandoibarra. In addition to the creation of neighbourhoods such as Miribilla, the revitalisation of Ametzola, the pedestrianisation of some streets in the centre and the gradual regeneration of the Old Bilbao, is the idea of a complete remodelling of the Zorrotzaurre peninsula. The Iraqi architect Zaha Hadid has been enlisted for this task.

The new neighbourhood of Miribilla built on old mining land.

Bilborock, the old Church of Merced –right–, the location in recent years of the Bilbao Pop-Rock Competition.

Michael Angelo's Moses in the Museum of Artistic Reproductions. ▶

LEISURE AND CULTURE

One of the most outstanding characteristics of 21st century Bilbao is its strong thrust as a cultural and leisure capital. In addition to the well-known **Guggenheim** and **Fine Arts Museums,** there are others such as the **Maritime, Taurine** and **Basque Museums** as well as that of **Reproducciones Artísticas** (Artistic Reproductions) and several art galleries and exhibition halls.

As far as music is concerned, the concerts organised by ABAO, **The Bilbao Association of Friends of Opera** are the most outstanding. More avid rock fans will enjoy those organised against very original backdrops such as **Azkena, Kafe Antzokia** and **Bilborock.** The latter is a convent converted into a multipurpose hall and in which the Concurso Pop-Rock Villa de Bilbao is held, the most interesting of its kind in Spain. Lovers of jazz, and other more daring styles, must not miss the **Bilbaína Jazz Club** programme. It is also worth highlighting the increased theatre variety both in the large scenarios of the **Arriaga Theatre** or the **Euskalduna Palace** as well as smaller and more alternative ones such as **La Fundición** (The Foundry). Along these lines, the effort made by **BAD,** the festival of dance and theatre, is worthy of mention.

Events such as the **Feria del Libro de Ocasión** (Opportunity Book Fair) and the **Festival de Cine Documental y Cortometraje** (Festival of Documental and Short Film Cinema) can be added to this list as well as others which lend a cultural flavour to the traditional business role of the town. All of the above has led to the inauguration of various hotels and catering and leisure establishments and shops with a markedly avant-garde hallmark. The new wave of immigration, especially from Africa and Latin America, has increased the number of restaurants with an ethnic flavour and bazaars of imported products. The homosexual community is helping to liven the image of the town as being increasingly diverse. The **Zinegoak International Festival of Gay-Lesbian-Transexual Cinema** is proof of this.

The people of Bilbao, regardless of how, enjoy socialising on the streets. In spite of a climate which is not always favourable, groups of friends meet to have a drink or snack and to eat *pintxos* in areas such as Licenciado Poza, Ledesma or the Seven Streets. The renowned Basque Gastronomy can be sampled in restaurants of acclaimed cuisine, cider houses, grillrooms and at attractive bars in pubs. Occasionally, and especially during the fiestas, groups of men can be overheard singing *bilbainadas,* the local song par excellence.

The town is at its most relaxed during the so-called Semana Grande de Agosto (Great Week of August), **Aste Nagusia,** during which concerts, theatre, fireworks, rural Basque sporting shows, circus events and bullfights abound. During this period, Bilbao appears to congregate, ready to party, along both sides of the **Arenal Bridge.**

The people of Bilbao also enjoy the fair of Santo Tomás, the day of San Blas, Santa Águeda, carnival and other festivities of a religious kind such as Semana Santa (Easter), which is increasingly viewed as rating amongst Spain's most famous.

Two bars in Bilbao, where delectable pintxos can be sampled.

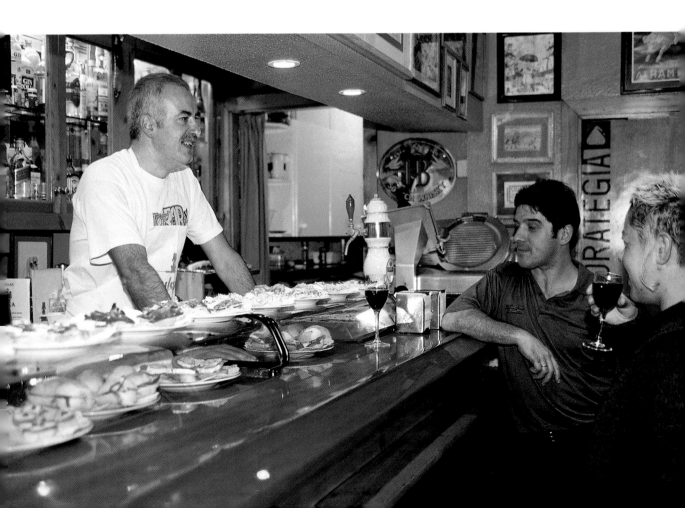

The Fair of Saint Tomás.

Traditional rowing boat on the estuary during the Bandera Villa de Bilbao regatta.

Left, the Gargantua "eats up" the children.

An "otxote", eight voices singing the traditional bilbainadas.

However, if there is something which unites all the inhabitants of the town, beyond social class and ideological struggles it is Athletic de Bilbao, the local football team. The team is virtually unique in the world in that only players from the region are accepted. This characteristic swells the pride of fans in Vizcaya and that of thousands of followers who support the club outside the Basque Country. It is worth walking round the outside of **San Mamés,** the football stadium referred to as The Cathedral, to become immersed in the atmosphere or visiting when a match is being played.

Finally, it must not be forgotten that the town is the centre of what is referred to as **Greater Bilbao** or, in its more ample and modern version, **Bilbao Metropolitano.** This group of thirty villages and towns is home to almost one million inhabitants, linked by a smooth network of communications and by many common objectives and projects.

The transfer of the **International Trade Fair** from its old location next to **San Mamés,** to **Barakaldo,** has also witnessed the creation, in the industrial locality, of a huge number of shopping centres and department stores. Without having to stray far from Bilbao it is recommendable visiting some beautiful villages such as **Getxo,** with its marvellous marina, **Portugalete,** with the famous **Puente Colgante** (Suspension Bridge), also known as **Puente de Bizkaia,** and beaches such as those in **Sopelana** and **Plentzia.**

The exemplary transformation of Vizcaya's capital has driven the development of the ring of municipalities surrounding it and, in general, of the province and the whole of the Basque Country.

Athletic fans cheering on the "lions" in San Mamés.

Inside the Trade Fair building.

*Outside the Trade Fair,
located in Barakaldo.*

Cranes of the Sestao shipyards, one of the estuary meanders with the most intense industry.

Below, the famous transporter bridge, called Puente Bizkaia, which joins both sides of the estuary.

Lighthouse and anchorage on the Arriluce quay.